FINISHING LINE PRESS

www.finishinglinepress.com

A Common Violence

poems by

Pat Falk

Finishing Line Press
Georgetown, Kentucky

By the Same Author:

Crazy Jane

It Happens As We Speak:
A Feminist Poetics

Sightings: Poems on Discovery

In the Shape of a Woman

A Common Violence

ACKNOWLEDGMENTS

Acknowledgement to the editors of *Eco-Poetry, The Examined Life Journal, Hyper
Texts, Long Island Quarterly, Long Island Sounds, The Mom Egg Review, Spillway
Literary Journal, The Suffolk Review, Third Wednesday: A Quarterly Journal of Poetry,
Prose and Art, Toward Forgiveness: An Anthology of Poems, VerseVirtual, Willows
Wept Review , WomenArts Quarterly Journal,* and *Xanadu Literary Journal,* in which
several of these poems first appeared.

In Memory

Adrienne Rich, Mentor and Literary Mother
Susan Bright, Poet and Publisher
Lee Wilson, My Mother

Special thanks to the following individuals: Pramila Venkateswaren, Kathrine
Jason, Sally Drucker, Richard Newman, Elaine Preston, Niamh P. Fitzgerald,
Candice Barenello, Gail Chapman, Mary Micelli, Linda Nicholson, Gloria
Wygand, David Padrusch, Janice Lyons Decker, Jane Roos, Jude Sunstrom,
Daniela Gioseffi, Denise Schlau, Regi Cabico, Marge Piercy, Denise Levertov,
Adrienne Rich, Patricia Monaghan, Molly Peacock, Annie Finch, Lois V. Walker.

Sincere thanks to my talented editor, Christen Kincaid.

Thank you, students.

My love to my daughter Karen, my granddaughter Maggie.

Publisher: Leah Maines
Editor: Christen Kincaid
Cover Art: Kristin Holcomb, kristinholcombphotography.com
Author Photo: Karen Stolberg
Cover Design: Christen Kincaid

Printed in the USA on acid-free paper.
Order online: www.finishinglinepress.com
                  also available on amazon.com

Author inquiries and mail orders:
Finishing Line Press
P. O. Box 1626
Georgetown, Kentucky 40324
U. S. A.

Table of Contents

3.
Laying Down Time

For Beth

In violence we forget who we are—*Mary McCarthy*

Even in the terrors of the night
there is a tendency toward grace that does not fail us—*Robert Goolrick*

barn's burnt down
now I can see the moon—*Mizuta Masahide*

1.

Rain

it's raining in Sudan, on farm grass, grain, and on the mules that carry water
from the nearby well

it's raining on the firewood, on carcasses of sheep and goats
that rot in marshy pools

it's raining on the mud brick huts, on thin straw walls held up with sticks
and lined with plastic sheeting

raining on the Janjaweed who laughing, shouting, fire pistols
deep into the darkened dawn

it's raining in Afghanistan, in Swaziland and Mozambique, the valley of Dredie

here in New York, on another side of pain,
I look out through my window to the yard next door

sheets and tee-shirts manufactured god knows where dangle
on a clothesline stretched from house to tree

my neighbor's at her ritual
hurried now against impending rain

she pulls and gathers, drops the items in
only once does she pause—her face turned fully to the wind—

then she carries the basket back into the house, into the light of day

A Common Violence

last night I slept in fits and bursts
                              rankled by the industry of dreams

a common violence in my genes
ever-raging

the stars misaligned
the planet cracking with abuse

                    I longed
for places unremembered and unseen

grant us grace I said   to whom or what   if never
peace then grace

Searchlight Over Gaza

for Izzeldin Abuelaish

seeking a language of peace

words conceived in darkness must be born in damp green moss
on beds of fern alone among acacia

alone among acacia under shade of eucalyptus and in leaves
the shape of hands unbending in the wind

words conceived in darkness must be born among the pine and in the clearing
where a few deer linger   foxes poised at attention

maybe those are searchlights in the grass or are they tired remnants of the stars

underfoot the crush of leaf
fog in all places and lightening in our bones

Regarding the Pain of Others

1.

they live in tents the thousands surviving the earthquake

a young girl pulled from the rubble hadn't died from impact
just her nails were missing   she must have scratched them off
trying to get out

2.

I wake this morning to a photo in *The New York Times*   a child in the street
his legs spread wide   a plaster cast on each

officials wanted information from his mother on his father—
a guerrilla in the mountains—

a man held the child's leg   two hands wound around
a tiny thigh and knee   snapped it like a chicken leg   then
the other

the mother watched as flesh turned purple   blood rising to the surface

3. Fahmi, Haditha

a roadside bomb then the carnage

        hard to piece together what transpired
who killed whom and when—

tortured—

Fahmi hid behind the curtain in his bedroom
heard the screams

        his neighbor
Younis Salim Khafif

pleading
for his life and for his daughters and his wife

and in the end
Fahmi told reporters

twenty four civilians

women shielding daughters
fourteen years of
ten years of five and three of
age and
one

slaughtered

4.

how to process this pain

what can help me not to see into that deep and cold inhuman space
where nature breaks in two green three green

white and yellow blackened leaves pushing through   the   dis- connect

Patriotic Discord

at the rally I notice dark birds

ravens, sparrows, crows that caw and caw
that circle the building   where poets speak
and politicians preach—

they flap their wings—
          they ride the wind moving righteously uptown
                    the wind bearing rhythms of words tapped out at the podium

their beaks— pointing in the same direction
as imaginary guns—   or real guns   we

are not safe my friend
this is how we know we are alive

News from the Shuttle

the earth is dying
we can see this from the spacecraft

deforestation
swirl of debris   and where there should be blue is grey haze
                            white electric non-light

humans we can't see are masked   :   :   inhale the noise of calloused want

we cannot make it through the outer layer   we report
the earth is less a home than somewhere else

Tanner Park

1.

a small house, municipal, set between two willows

where it faces the bay a weathered deck
collapses into sand

prop yourself
against the wall   read   think   walk easily
through piled weed and sea grass

this is where I want to die

those final hours
crumpled in a chair at water's edge
        a passing gull as witness

2.

the beach has changed

the house
and trees are gone
a sprawling white pavilion in their stead

a boardwalk, fishing pier
and promenade stretch out into the bay

3.

a child digs beneath a pine
without much effort   dry earth
severed roots
        clumped with grass and needles

the woman with him seems distracted, shields herself
from the wind's debris—

this is dirt, she knows, not sand in her eyes
she does not name formaldehyde chlorine and dust of asphalt

4.

does a machine have spirit
does it hover over carcasses of antiquated engines abandoned on the beach

particles of rusted metal carried in the wind
to lodge in sand and lung

5.

walking over burning sand
where once were stones and shells and weed

sea glass—

now the sand
is simply smooth the sand is simply burning in the sun's unholy glare

6.

the water is warm in the shallows
warm too in the not supposed to be tampered with depths

algae on the surface   oily film of green blue red give it a name
this shore without a sea   this landscape

seascape   objects burning in the sun's white glare

where stones in our pockets
pull us down

where messages rise like steam   like belief

Slick

it's the day past groundhog's day
when the sun   in a rare mid-winter passion

has stretched itself to six o'clock   cut through the clouds
overtaken trees

I visited the beach today
for the rush and pull of an old familiar friend

to walk among the weathered gulls   along the winding shore
but the sea was black and all the sea gulls dead

Three Bits

1. Chickens

>the twister took
>them up   then hundreds
>tumbled
>down
>naked   every feather
>ripped out
>in the wind
>
>it was raining
>plucked chickens

2. Canada Geese

>they flew
>through a cloudless sky
>into the clear green glass of a massive building
>
>those struck senseless
>after landing
>shook
>
>themselves   back up
>and with a quiet flutter flew
>off
>
>others
>with shattered skulls
>and broken necks
>became
>dinner

3. Rabbits

This one still hurts.
They were to test effects of toxic bleach:
the eyelids of the rabbits stitched open.

Sky Watch

overhead a swarm of birds, screaming, squabbling—

I didn't know that birds in flight could sound so human
one, a gull, is holding in its beak

something long and furry
fox-like—
small legs dangling looking like those of a dog

in the seagull's eye
malevolence
the arrogance of a master race

other gulls and geese—jealous or enraged—
pursuing from behind

Homing

Amityville Bay Beach

A cage in the parking lot filled with birds. A man with long legs
and narrow chest sets them free.

White doves rise above the bay flapping and squawking,
then gather in formation
out to sea.
                                        Always a miracle how they know.
To fly, to form, and to go home.

I would like to go home.
And hope it isn't death itself that brings me there.   Home in my body.
Home in someone's arms.   Home in mystery.

And to get there after letting go. For decades I have done the work.
My daughter leaving.   Lovers dying.   October leaves skittling over dry grass.

At Aunt Eva's gravesite the rabbi explains: turn the shovel over, curved
side facing up. Scoop the earth, balance, carry, toss and walk away.

Meaning *this is something I don't want to do but mus*t.

Sixty pigeons grace the sky.
Today's flight: eighty miles to the east.

Snail

1.

appearing as always after the rain
on the sidewalk

body softwet grey
neck and head stuck out in brazen vulnerability

front-forked antenna
shell
of alternating cream colored/dark brown/broad stripes
        long wormy tail

it must be taken back into the garden

2.

I try a five-fingered leaf
slipped beneath the palpitating grey
just a nudge
not to rip the underbelly—

                        still the fierce resistance—
head snaps in   tail slaps back
            and all the huddled rest of it
                    rooted
                        to the burning asphalt

3.

water poured
around it from a cup

brings the tiny monster-head
to drink

full of trust and puddled now
it floats
             with ease
                        ontotheleaf

There is Nothing I have Buried that Can Die

Storm-beaten, tough-winged passenger
there is nothing I have buried that can die

Adrienne Rich

day night   dark/light
neither overtakes nor cheats nor gives a damn about power

the earth
spins with the clarity

and poise
of a small bird perched

exactly on a branch where needed

*

before long vision is fractured
balance upended

concrete abstraction
torn to bits

the twig remains a twig
the sky a house to the clouds

but the bird's gone
before we can give it a name

*

December 7
dark this morning

a patch of light burns violently
through pitch

everywhere the innocent are dreaming
some still sleeping

others folding clothing
bathing—

some are fighting off or fighting back

*

blame is odorless and sticks to the tongue
is utterly useless

if we are human / as we are / you say
we are to raise a hand

inside
the mind   palm pressed flatly open to the world

light in the palm
code in the bone   wrist flexed bending where is gathered

wisdom   beyond capacity for harm

*

where have you gone   Adrienne
what's to be done

when your life
closed

a tree fell—
the impact felt

by thousands of your daughters
and your sons

when your life closed
I mourned a mother more

a mother than
my own

*

you have my words   you told me in a dream
you have my word   I heard

on waking

you held me gave me water had me
rest my head

my mind
a tooth   I cut   on wood

my voice
a voice of many   yours—

*

the day Anne Sexton took her life
we walked across the campus

you spoke
of women poets   what

we need to do
you were limping   I was reading

speaks of the fault that sends me limping

they'll fuck you up
you said

we went inside the building

no they won't
I said

I read you wrote
you spoke   I heard

there's nothing I have buried that can die

*

tonight the birds are scattered
in the trees around

the lake

they are white herons
hanging

like ornaments
from

the branches

they have come
from all across the island

have flown
inland from the sea

they form a silent
border

settle
peaceably

will stay the night
lit by a beacon

somewhat like the moon

2.

Songbird Landing

1.

imagine
      a songbird

returning after long silence—

      imagine a city   of chrome
and glass and polished

stone—

blinded by the light   reflected
off the river

how

will she manage
to land

and where

2.

I am walking to the rhythm of an old song

a song of rain—of trees in fog—
of rustling

weathered branches

but like a dream that changes in the telling

the song keeps changing
in the singing

and this seemingly endless
          walking

3.

best to rest   in small grey pauses
mossy pockets   raindrops still
                        on fallen leaves

the song prolongs   note by note by slow
clear note   the fog lifting

songbird landing   here

Through a Wall Darkly

she gazes through a glass wall that opens to the sea
a piano in the corner of the room

why so alone   you'd think
that if the soul had any sense she would invite a friend
or someone from the family

well this one needs her space

aware of something *other*   out there
untouched and to be touched
when the sky splits open and the dark round stones of the earth come home

Barometric

low pressure before a storm
sends me reeling—the entire earth perhaps—

with knowledge of impending violence

carried through a synapse
down the spine
into hollow open pockets

the soul goes underground, a dusty bulb
in a pit of darkness

how deceptive this darkness   *I am comfort and safety*
it says   *I am the promise of renewal*

(if we don't sink down
into depression on our own
it will rise up and grab us, pull us in)

the month is March—the wind—
the wind moves all

Household

the house is speaking: rest, read, watch tv
clean up the mess from last night's rage
the cracked bowl, shattered glass

all I ever wanted was protection
solid walls against the sting of winter
a window to see through
imagine a life beyond myself

the house is breathing, or is it song?
the house believes it is God

Hanukah, No Miracle

All nine candles must completely burn
before I leave the house.

I could blow them out
let the thin grey smoke drift with the draft
but that may bring bad luck, like undoing all the wishes
made on recent birthdays.

I could leave the candles burning
but I'd have visions
of my dog catching fire, or the drapes.

So I wait and watch the blue green red white
drip and disappear. I read a poem by Ahkmatova
called "Astonishment"
and think of stars
and stones
and listen to the *click tick click*
of the second-hand clock.

What is depression?
Too many candles—one is too many
a thousand not enough.

Quickening

I saw the winter sun before I saw the snow,
my gaze falling slowly past the geese, the passing gulls,
past the dark hard trees gleaming and heavy,
falling on the river where buffleheads and canvasbacks
converge in scattered patterns—an image so bright, so stunning,
it seemed a photograph, or memory, of love.

We are standing by the still cold water,
the ice floes breaking and reshaping
as the splintered pieces drift downstream. How is it
that we know—for we do know—that no matter how desolate
our lives may seem, the sun will sink into our deepest pockets
where we sleep and breathe, remember, then begin again.

Soul

in the dream I was blind
and out of the darkness
you emerged
spirit and substance
psyche
and form   :   :

standing seagulls face the wind
sometimes
they balance
on one foot   the other
tucked

into a feathered belly :   :

in the dream
you promised to stay   even after
I woke up   tell me
how many gulls

inhabit the beach in a lifetime

Black Pearl

black pearls are not black at all

aqua and deep green   glint of violet—
as if they stole their colors

from the wings
of a starling lit by the moon   my love

is truly not a love he   is a black pearl

on the road of someone else's purpose

on the road of someone else's purpose
I shudder to a stop   the night sky clear

as last time I was here

the same startling silence
same chill   near frost   sudden

glint of starlings   sunk in moonlit
snow

old age needs no invitation

old age needs no invitation

bones function or break   blood runs its course
driven by a heart that will one day fail

sixteen years ago I was middle-aged
sixteen years from now I will be elderly if alive

even now my hands' veins are gnarled like roots
breasts flattened back against my ribs

old age uninvited spreads like newsprint on my lap

where the three ponds meet

you can find me where the three ponds meet
where they merge like petals into one blue body
where goldfish on the surface scuttle luminescently
slipping after sundown into cooler, darker, depths

when the pond freezes in winter, do the fish freeze too?
or do they find their way below the growing ice
protected on the ever-fluid floor—as all of us
as nights grow colder sleep so deeply

we forget ourselves and thus the fear of death,
a fear begun when shadows lengthened into evening,
the questions swimming out of reach
into the thickening roiling blue

Lost in Cold Spring Harbor

A road of pitch and sudden bend,
of soft snow swirling, of sunlight thrumming
strobe-like through the twisted limbs of winter trees;
these are blue trees, brown trees, black
and some with crusted ice on pitted ruts of bark.

Dizzy from the peaks and dips and flickering light,
I shift too quickly into second gear along a steep incline
nearly skidding off a cliff. I don't know
where I am nor where I'm going and so truly lost
in all this beauty do not care.

I'm climbing back up north then east again,
Then down into the dense and dreamy harbor.

Code Orange

a woman too old to be in the room
is in this poem
she's the salt of the earth   (mountain rain (snow, fall-
out))
jewel of the mind   find her

it may mean climbing through a window
at the close of day to the other side
to fresh air   where the sun shines
and animals—

a bridge   a small
stream slipping over stones   —belly, ark—

    and in the dream she wore grey
        a long skirt spilling to the floor
            silk blouse, breasts apparent
      through metallic film and sequins
        a silver braided chain

give me her   dampen the intensity
      of sense: television,
          newsprint, casualties of war

give me
her   silver spear glinting in the midnight sun
le coeur of the cobra
bloodsuck, tuck this heart
and breath a warm June breeze
and know—who now born again—kingly oh so kind

For Maggie, Not Yet Born

> *and Maggie discovered a shell that sang*
> *so sweetly she couldn't remember her troubles*

E.E. Cummings

someday you will tell them
how I came to you

the cool night air
outside your mother's body

opened

I stood beside her said *goodbye, drive safely*

her car parked beside the pond
a slight mist rising

drive safely—
there may be fog along the road

my arms embracing, hands barely meeting
as we hugged

she was so large in the middle with you

then her body opened like a shell—the kind you hear the ocean in—

I heard that hidden ocean
imagined you within it

floating
swimming with the tide and against the tide

Maggie, someday you will tell them how I took your hand

inside that dark and airy place
and left with you

a part of me
something even I don't know

I have—had—nothing I can see or feel—
but you will know it, see it, say it

Maggie, daughter of my daughter

you will know
exactly what it is I give you

now—

Maggie and Me in the Garden

The ground half cleared, thorny shoots cut down
and withered bulbs pulled out. Maggie sees
that she and I are just like all of life.

I am old, I say, my skin wrinkled like the leaves,
and I am new! she laughs, a flash of joy in her eyes.

Something good about our hands digging deeply into earth,
pulling and longing, cutting and cleaning;
everything seems to be singing
and we are the song.

Cobolt

for Karen

A blue ceramic bowl sits exactly where we placed it
in the center of a table thirty years ago. You were seven,
I at thirty-five a single mother sure that by
example you would thrive.

I touch the rim as if it were a memory,
my finger circling slowly with a tenderness
I may have never had to give you.   Could I not see
beyond the need for strength?

And what to give you now, daughter, grown fierce and rent,
bent fully in the pit of struggle.

I want to smash that bowl in all its cobalt denseness—
dye, sand, mud, clay—reduce to truth
what splinters, softens, matters
still/what seems to
matter not at all.

Grandma Sadie

She had a round face and thick white hair.
Her loose skin rippling when she'd lift an arm,
hands trembling reaching for the jam.
Mostly I saw fear in grandma's eyes, sometimes shifting
into softened kindness.

She knew no English, nor I the Russian
of her mother tongue.
She taught me phrases such as *diamon ya't kopek*,
a penny in my palm if I said it right.

She died in a home for the elderly infirm
a year after grandpa—woman beater, vodka drinker,
large gruff man—who in the cramped back bedroom
of their Brooklyn railroad flat, according to my mother
would beat and rape my Sadie.

I have cursed him at his grave.

gration)

urn every winter to inhabit the pond
ds of wrens huddled on ice
ls & sparrows in greygangs & brownwhite clusters

then that I hear my mother's voice
k at those birds!

ears ago she stayed with me when she flew up north from Boca
in the afternoon she'd take a nap
wake to have another drink, get dressed and leave the house

one day she opened the door
said *look at those birds!*

it was more than a statement, not quite a demand
an affirmation of our love of all things aviary—
so beautiful and fleeting, fragile and free

free to murder, free to leave

Memory, You

Two lifetimes tangled like old trees knotted by pain.

This image is mine, I own this forest, this country.
I have tried to keep you out, have pushed back memories like flattened eggs
hatching daily.

There have been four or five good ones, memories, in fifty-eight years.
Some I have distorted, it's true, but there's a book that doesn't lie in every soul.

You can make a graph of it—a few lines rising up, several crashing down.
At some point the pen goes through the paper stabbing or burning as if through
  skin.

Her Words

My mother said it doesn't matter if a woman comes or not.
It does, though, for a man—a backup of his sperm
will make his balls ache, he will get sick.
It seemed that women had to suck, blow, spread their legs,
push, pull, prod, do whatever was demanded
to disgorge the swollen manhood.
I imagined backed-up rivers, tiny fish trampled at the delta,
plankton turned to stone, to pebbles hard and raging.

Now my mother's old and sick and dying.
I wonder if she ever fully lived, given her take on love.
I wish her well. I wish her peace. But most of all
I wish she'd take that pack of lies back into the grave with her.
Had I believed her (but how could I believe her?)
maybe I'd have loved her and her weird and wicked ways;
I learned instead to love myself,
to live in cool blue darkness, on fire and alone.

Reflections by a River

It's been a brutal winter
several trees died
even evergreens and strong broad oaks
                              cracked in the cold

now as every spring
the mute swan
flaunts
incessant reproduction

        some eggs hatch   some dead matter floating

this is the year my mother will die
it's been   at times   a painful life
for her
for me

I pull apart the tangled threads   filaments
        and splintered twigs
                oak from pine, leaf from weed
                      tall grass from soft warm earth

the lights are dim at dusk along the river
dim as well at dawn

Rehearsal

I imagine my mother's death.

The phone will ring, I'll pick it up, glancing at the number on caller ID.
My sister, perhaps, or my mother's husband Donald. Florida. *Mommy—
your mother—died last night.*

Will I feel then as I do now, rehearsing? The simple relief of her passing
after wishing it for so long. Or the quick smack of guilt.

One knife slipping out, another one in.

Our love is physical and spiritual, I can hear her say. The last time we spoke
she demanded I tell her I love her.

I responded in the abstract, something about genes and passages, tunnels
and time.

Does the ocean love the sky?
The desert the volcano that deposits ash, stone, sludge into every sacred space?
The phone will ring. I will pick it up. And I will cry.

My Mother's Death in Autumn

1.

the trees are walking out of themselves
like shadow out of form
you can hear them breathe if you listen well and long

they rim the lake
with necessary death
leaves of
scarlet
amber   green
some still
clinging
falling
finally into matted thickness

2.

an aged oak is dying
her mottled
bark
crumbling
like malignant
bone

her tangled roots
abandoned
to a vast
indifferent earth

sometimes when the wind blows
she will respond
her voice
muffled
her spirit nearly gone

you can hear her breathe if you listen well and long

3.

yesterday a herd of deer gathered by the lake
not far from where the oak once stood
I gave them apples—
breadcrumbs to the crows that hovered in the trees—   then came more
crows descending like a cloud

4.

and then they were gone
and then it was winter
bright with sun

Requiem

for Beth

you are smooth and round
a statue spun of radiant stone, glint of diamond, opal, pearl

an iron tree in bloom
your roots in conversation with the soil

you are the other side of silence, a distant star of icy flame
an arc of death above a continent of grief

I hear you now, my friend, like silenced Philomela
speaking with your eyes, your hands

working through the too long night, wanting to write,
to write, wanting

deciding finally to live as if the poems would write themselves
then rise into the air like birds, like song

sister, poet, my dear beloved Beth—this poem
is filled with nightingales—

the grief is mine, the song forever yours

3.

Laying Down Time

* * *

Now I lay me down to sleep
I pray the earth my soul to keep
If I should die before I wake...

* * *

*Adenocarcinoma of the lung is the growth of abnormal cells that multiply
out of control and form a tumor. As it grows, the tumor destroys parts of
the lung and can spread throughout the body. Localized, it may respond
better than other lung cancers to treatment, especially surgical removal
of the tumor.*

1.

I sit among the trees and breathe
if I were a tree, I wouldn't need to think
to breathe, or unthink

beneath the tree I am protected
my shoulders drop my belly swells
air rises to my lungs and greets the dawn

what will be cut from me is of no consequence
what will remain will be healed   I am a reed
I am at peace, I want this cancer out

2.

morning begins at night in winter
day begins when first light
burns through pitch

small solace in such frigid air

there is something to be said for ritual
like folding clothing
edge-to-edge

or opening a book of poems
the pages flattened out in meaning

I am not ready for this darkness
not nearly ready—no—
for death

3.

a night broken by wonder
did the moon speak…

the mist off the ocean
dampen the sheet…

we ought to sleep as cattle
with questions dissolved

and nothing
but clouds in our eyes

how to learn to do this
to lay down fear with time

4.

leave the sheep sleeping
their dreams are merely echoes
in their own internal chambers

quiet now, listen to the wild one
who calms herself then slips
unnoticed past the guards

and who am I, you ask, the voice
that speaks to you now? I find you
in your dreams and lead you out to safety

I intercede, make things smooth,
make things make their own
things in a good way

5.

morning brings the violent fear
immediately from sleep

it's felt as movement   heat through stone

beneath my bed an old dull knife
dulled by decades of disuse

a box of dusty flat grey stones—
to throw—or hold—

they say the mind can heal itself
a glass of water

in a room of bolted doors

6.

light rain this morning
front steps dark with wet   I need to change
and to be changed: every cell calling out
it's time, it's time, it's time

the swan on her nest is not always still
sometimes she picks at her feathers
stretches her neck to dig out reeds
stands to turn an egg

mostly, though, the rain and sun
beat down on her
there must be a core that protects her
a *chi* that lies deep within

7.

time, that old sweet snake,
makes a rolling wave kind of motion
mountain after mountain
each one proclaiming its importance

would that time lay down as a smooth soft shaft

        I am standing
in a wind that says *lay down*
lay down lay down
listen to the heartbeat
of the earth and know it not
for the call of death—
though that will come in its own
sweet time—

but the world will render back at last
your unclaimed soul long
hidden in the dark

sweet snake, sweet soul, lay down now with time
breathe with the grasses and the reeds

be the rod thou art
be the rod   the art

8.

all this work to get to the place where love abides
crossing the border past the guards

cutting through the thicket to an old house in the mountains

the rooms to explore, exchanges to make
parts of the self transacted
and what relief to lay down arms
          every bone gone soft, the hair lying quietly in place

9.

the tree by my pond is full of leaves
except for the shock   of bare dead limbs

jutting out at several angles

a tangle of wood in the daylight
by evening half obscured

in leafy thickness

in moonlight just a group of sticks
lit by the soul

Notes

For Beth: my dedication is to Beth Fein, dear friend and wonderful poet, born in 1961, who left us in 2007. Her ashes were scattered in Montauk, a place where she had written "Montauk—2003;" she declares, "Somewhere here I live… Somewhere here the wind and rain pass through me to the ground./ Somewhere here, somehow here/I wait to be told it is time to leave."

"Regarding the Pain of Others": The title is from Susan Sontag, *Regarding the Pain of Others*. Farrar, Straus and Giroux; First Edition, February 19, 2002. *The New York Times* article referred to begins with a front page photo and caption describing violence inflicted on a Zimbabwean child (June 16, 2008 edition), though in an editors' note of July 9, 2008, a correction indicated that the 11 month old boy's legs were in casts as treatment for club feet; upon examination, the baby's legs showed no evidence of bone fractures. Nevertheless, the mother and others contend that the baby was thrown to the floor by youths supporting Mugabe, and that desperation led the mother to fabricate the story in order to seek help.

"News from the Shuttle": See "Shuttle Views the Earth: Human Imprints from Space," Gwynn, David W. and Wilkinson, M. Justin; Lulla, Kamlesh P. http://www.lpi.usra.edu/publications/slidesets/humanimprints/index.shtml

"Nothing Buried That Can Die" (*for Adrienne Rich*)
speaks of the fault that sends me limping from Adrienne Rich, "Waking in the Dark" *there's nothing I have buried that can die* from Adrienne Rich, "Calle Vision"

"Laying Down Time" epigram *adenocarcinoma…tumor* is a description from http://www.intelihealth.com/IH/ihtIH/c/9339/24402.html

Pat Falk is Professor Emeritus at SUNY's Nassau Community College in Garden City, New York where she teaches writing and literature. She's the author of two other collections of poetry, *In the Shape of a Woman,* and *Crazy Jane;* the literary memoir, *It Happens As We Speak: A Feminist Poetics;* and she edited the anthology *Sightings: Poems on Discovery.* Her work has been widely reviewed; *The American Book Review* calls her writing "visionary," saying she has created "a new language."

She has received awards from *Creative Nonfiction,* National League of American Pen Women, The National Writer's Voice Project, *Many Mountains Moving, Black Bear Review,* and the Pushcart Press, along with two SUNY Faculty Distinguished Achievement Awards, a CUNY fellowship, a Vermont Studio Center Writer's Grant, and SUNY's Chancellor's Award for Creative Work.

Her work has appeared in several literary journals including *The New York Times Book Review, Thirteenth Moon, The Mickle Street Review,* and *Women Artists News.* Her research and activism concern human rights, global ecology, and the integrity of all life in the industrial and institutional settings. Originally from Queens, New York, she lives on the south shore of Long Island.

Visit her website at patfalk.net

Praise for Pat Falk's Work:

Crazy Jane

Visionary...resolutely uplifting, validating, and gratifying. —*American Book Review*

Implacable powerfulness which the poet conveys starkly and seductively. —*Poets' Quarterly*

A truly unique and honest voice in American poetry. —*Wheelhouse Magazine*

Moves [the] reader through individuality of voice and its compression of idea & physical world. —Adrienne Rich

In the Shape of a Woman

Written with a quiet fortitude...Falk brings us into her world with raw, gutsy detail and without apology." —*Book/Mark*

Falk...speaks to the heart of anyone who views their life as a continuing process of conscious refinement. —*Long Island Update*

What the attentive reader feels is an ethereal sense of intimacy—an almost ineffable identification with the persona's humanity...the writer artfully commands our unreserved confidence. —*New York Beacon*

Truly breathtaking and erotic and real. —Regie Cabico

It Happens as We Speak: A Feminist Poetics

Creates new language... transcend[ing] one individual's quest by vividly portraying an era familiar to many of us. —*American Book Review*

A book of of birth, and life, and change, and wisdom. —Alicia Ostriker

A riveting mix of candor and musing. —Molly Peacock

A moving read. —Annie Finch

Affirms the value of poetry as a means of spiritual enlightenment. —Daniela Gioseffi